GRAIL

IF I WERE TO...

SWARNIKA

ISBN 979-888546509-0

If I were to...

Contents

Contents

Contents

Preface

"Grail: If I were to..." is a unique anthology that houses 40 poems by 14 poets. All these poems are unique in the sense that they all begin with the fragment "If I were to". These marvels of poetry run across various themes and ideas. All the poets were given the choice to write a piece of poetry as per their will, with the only condition being that it should initiate with the given fragment. This Anthology exhibits the scope of writing even when conditioned or constrained.

All pieces of poetry in this anthology are original pieces by the poets and they ensure that these haven't been published anywhere before.

This anthology has been edited and compiled by Swarnika. This project has been sponsored by Nrityangana Kala Kendra OPC Private Limited.

Acknowledgements

I'd like to express my deep appreciation and admiration to all the co-authors of this anthology. They have added value to this anthology just like how colors add gravity to a picture. The project wouldn't have been the same without their contribution. The project has been initiated by Nrityangana Kala Kendra OPC Private Limited. All contributions are sincerely appreciated and gratefully acknowledged.

All the poems in this anthology are original pieces by our co-authors. No set of words can amount to my appreciation for our co-authors- Putul Mangni Mandal, Dr. Rakesh Kumar Singh, Gauri Shukla, Raman Singh, Khushi Kaushik, Jeevasha Batra, Rahul Jha, Shruti Upadhyay, Ananya Dutta, Tushita Aster Paul, Akrita, Nishita Sharma and Ritika Tyagi. I'd forever be indebted to them.

Prologue

If I were to be...

....

If I were to be,
I would have probably been.

....

I would have probably been
What I wanted to be.

....

What I wanted to be,
But couldn't be...

....

If I were to be
I would have probably been;
What I wanted to be,
But couldn't be.

....

- Swarnika

Co-Authors of the Book

Swarnika

Putul Mangni Mandal

Dr. Rakesh Kumar Singh

Gauri Shukla

Raman Singh

Khushi Kaushik

Jeevasha Batra

Rahul Jha

Shruti Upadhyay

Ananya Dutta

Tushita Aster Paul

Akrita

Nishita Sharma

Ritika Tyagi

Nrityangana Kala Kendra

(OPC) Private Limited

Nrityangana Kala Kendra (OPC) Private Limited is a company started by Miss Swarnika for the education of various art forms along with the promotion of extra-curricular activities. The company deals with research and exploration in the various forms of art as well. For different forms of dance, art and music, there are yearly certification programs that come with monthly examination. There are research groups along with performance troops organised from time to time. Language and literature are chiefly appreciated and endeavoured. The company collaborates and initiates ideas that are later compiled and published as books with the efforts of the team. The company also aims to start competitions and functions for artists of all ages to showcase their talent and get felicitated for the same.

Nrityangana Kala Kendra was started as to keep the classical roots of Bharatnatyam and Kathak alive, but with time the company broadened its horizon to encompass other art forms as well. The company also organises skill-enhancement courses and workshops every now and then.

Swarnika

Swarnika is an avid reader and an ambivert. She is a glass-half-full kind of a person, not because she is always an optimist but because she believes that a glass that is full has no more scope and ends up creating the most amount of spills.

She completed her Bachelor's and Master's degree from the University of Delhi. She has completed her three-level professional certification in Spanish language from Valencia Polytechnic University, Spain. She has also completed her certificate program in French language from St. Stephen's College, University of Delhi. She is currently pursuing a Post-Graduate Diploma in Business Administration from Symbiosis Centre for Distance Learning, Pune. She is working on her thesis and research papers to earn her Ph.D. degree in English Literature.

She has a keen interest in criminology and detective fiction.
Writings that indulge mystery and rationale speak volumes to her.
She has earned her TEFL and TESOL certificates as an English
language teacher. She is also a certified dance teacher with
specializations in Bharatnatyam, Kathak, and Contemporary. She is
also certified in Classical Music and Fine Arts.

She exhibits abundant admiration for food and would call herself a foodie. She believes in living in the moment rather than giving the moment the opportunity to live through you without you even realizing it. She has started her company- Nrityangana Kala Kendra OPC Private Limited on her own. She has been tutoring kids along with mentoring graduate and postgraduate students in academic and creative writing.

On some days she is a dreamer while on others she is a realist. She firmly believes in humanism. Nature mesmerizes her. On a usual day, you'd find her curled up in a corner either with a book or watching a movie/episode while relishing food.

She has initiated this project and has edited the book along with compiling it.

1. Burning Roses

If I were to tell you
A tale of two today,
Promise you'll keep it a secret
By sharing it along the way.

....

The buds of the day
Eved at bloom,
Grand-minute stars traveled
In ecstasy and in gloom.

....

The blooming roses cross paths
The moment gets still,
The sun kisses the moon
Passing by the hill.

....

The tides are low tonight
As the flames get high,
All beginnings meet their end
Sighs the lunar sky.

....

A petal falls off one rose
Undressed by the blowing breeze,

GRAIL

As it falls, it touches the stem
Embracing the moments to seize.

....

The prolonged touch starts a fire
Another moment passes by,
Consumed by their fate and desire
Burned the roses under the lunar sky.

– Swarnika

2. Miss Cruelty

If I were to tell you about her,
I would be worried as to where to start.
As I put the conundrum into words,
It is my soul that would depart.

....

Her eyes were bright like the sun,
They burnt my soul alive.
As radiant was her smile,
Blinded me forever to strife.

....

I heard that melody,
The melody that was her voice.
I was enchanted
And I knew it came with a price.

....

This melody in my ears,
Drummed to my heart.
I might be able to rhyme now,
But no more to be heard.

....

As I walked past
Her whiff caught me off-guard.

I forgot to breathe since then
From it once, now into the earth.

....

I can't hear and I was unheard,
I couldn't see and I was unseen.
My words etched in a shriek,
For I lost my voice to that evil queen.

....

I felt nothing,
And none could feel me.
The shattered heart was buried,
Under the giant oak tree.

- Swarnika

Putul Mangni Mandal

Putul Mangni Mandal is a Postgraduate student who feels that writing is a sublime experience. She's a keen observer and curious child ready with a blank slate to chalk down every detail of life.

Having been born into a small family with a small income living in a big city, Delhi, she often faces very basic challenges in life. But when it's too much, she slips into deep meditations. In the dark fluid passages of mind, she often finds the chintz of light scattered everywhere like little Krishna has opened his mouth just for her. So placing the warm palms on her face, when she tries to burn the impression down on her soul and opens her eyes, often she is endowed with a poem. She's been doing it for about seven years but now as she's become aware that many might share in her feelings, through a string of some of her poems, she'd like to sit beside some souls to make sure they're not alone.

3. A Substitute

If I were to have a substitute for my past
I'd replace it with a syllabus.
So like a graduate who finished
The greatest tragedies hastily
Blaming shortage of time,
I'd dig it out again
From the unconscious shelf
And skim down to the past
when you were breathing alive.
I'd relish soliloquies this time
That protagonists often screech,
And the sermons too
The writers gradually beseech.
I'd highlight dialogues
And will use them as quotes,
Will try to understand characters too.
But for the forlorn events,
I'd leave a leaf for remembrance.
Although the course would be over.

- Putul Mangni Mandal

4. Carry a Message

If I were to free my desires
from the shackles of my ambitions,
I would ask them
to carry a message too,
to the unseen nooks of lives
where in the withered houses,
thrives the sorriest memories.

....

I would beg them
to become a next day
where a day seems to end,
to rain down onto the impotent soils,
to grow in the impossible wombs,
to flow under the sun when it boils.
to spread like a rainbow over the pouring eyes,
to come across a face like a smile bloom,
or become Eureka in a scientist's mind
and develop into a vaccine soon.

....

Please go, you seem the only way out
for I believe that not all paths are dark yet!
Not all the desires are harmed yet!

And not all the hopes are charmed yet!

– Putul Mangni Mandal

5. It

If I were to save someone
it would be a lizard.

....

Has it ever harmed anyone?

....

But

....

O Frightened O brave, you children!
Poke at it with brooms and sticks
Whichever is handy.
That poor little creature
that doesn't even have bones!
On the ceilings and to the walls
you chase.
It runs.
It hides.
You say it creeps you?
It scares you?

....

You say it invades?
It's foreign?
It's a disease?

SWARNIKA

It was there all your life.
Did you notice?

....

Well it will stay there.
You will see.
So
back to the point, you go
where a circle starts.

- *Putul Mangni Mandal*

6. The Girl

If I were to tell that girl…
Often who visits.
Often she impales my eyes
Only to find my conscious
Busy with the new memories.
Often she sadly returns
On not finding a certain piece.

…. …. …. ….

If I were to tell that girl…
The odds that life carries.
The potentials it has,
The magic and faeries.
Like a constant flow
It has to go on
And stop? No!
Till the stones become sand
And sand become slit
And to further numerous forms
It's going to hit.
It's a fact!

…. …. …. ….

Only if I were able to dare,

I would break the mirror,
Give her an embrace,
And tell her not to care.

....
If I were to tell that girl.

- *Putul Mangni Mandal*

Dr. Rakesh Kumar Singh

Dr. Rakesh Kumar Singh is currently working as Assistant Professor in Zakir Husain Delhi College(Evening), University of Delhi. He has done M.A in Philosophy from the University of Delhi where he topped the university. He has done M.Phil and Ph.D. in Philosophy from Jawaharlal Nehru University, Delhi where he worked on some very important issues of Continental Philosophy. Before teaching at this place he has taught in Jawaharlal Nehru University, Amity Institute of Psychology and Allied Sciences, and some other colleges of the University of Delhi. He has contributed several articles for different national and international journals. Recently he is working on "Phenomenology of Silence" and "Heidegger and Anaximander fragment".

7. If I Were To Be An Enlightened Person

If I were to be an enlightened person
I would have devoted my life
on study and meeting people
from all over the world
with some good reason.

....

I would have tried to convince people
not to fight on religion.
But to understand spirituality
which is in giving an opportunity
of Nirvaan to everyone.

....

I would have tried to rewrite the books of
Politics, Society and Economics
with a concept of "other/Other"
Which is in its alterity
towards the infinite/anant

....

If I were an enlightened person
I would have tried to solve

all the unsolved problems of the world
and especially those
which cause blood, apathy and
kill all the reason.

....

I would have tried to think on
all the basic problems of life
with the problems of greed,
Simulacra and all the Simulations.

....

I would have tried to say----
EACH ONE TEACH ONE and the
FOOD FOR EVERYONE
with an emphasis on
Knowledge, nous and art
to create a spark of practical wisdom.

....

If I were an enlightened person
I would have tried to translate
all the great books of the world
into a vernacular notion.

....

I would have tried to make
this earth a better place to live
with a sense of ecological peace
where beauty is not only outside
but also in mind

and the contemplation on
Truth, Ethics, and Sublime
become possible for everyone.

....

I would have tried to say that there is bliss
in respecting women
and the old people.
Life does not have any meaning
without virtue
and so the capacity build-up
is the main thing of education.

....

I have many wishes; many problems.
But I am unable to do any of them
Because I lack alethia.
Yet there is aporia.
I can only wish....

....

....

If I were an enlightened person.
If I were an enlightened person.

- Dr. Rakesh Kumar Singh

8. If I Were To Be An Event In The Zone Of Thinking

If I were to be an event in the zone of thinking
I would have asked this question
to the dwelling of Being.
How does it come into Becoming
with an infinite flow of creation
and all these happenings?
Is there any meaning
or it is an absurd dreaming?
How does it distribute Possibility
if everything is scattering?
Time is waiting
and the Call is none.
Is there anywhere Truth
which could activate Self /Agency
with a sense of other
and all these beings?

… … … …

.. … … …
If I were an event in the zone of thinking

I would have asked this question
to the dwelling of Being.

– Dr. Rakesh Kumar Singh

Gauri Shukla

Gauri Shukla is a third year Literature student pursuing her passion for reading and writing from the University of Delhi. President of the Literary Society of the college, she is an avid reader who yearns to get lost in estranged, galvanic worlds of art. A national level debater, she is someone who doesn't shy away from speaking her mind. An ardent scripturient, she has written articles for The Times of India, Women's Republic, The Hindu, The Redstockings Chronicles, etc. She's currently working on a South-Asian anthology as an editor alongside editors from Bangladesh and Pakistan. Her lifelong dream is to document experiences and sentiments of different people, belonging to different cultures, all around the world. She believes life is too short and time is fleeting thus, each moment needs to be savored and felt to its optimum level. She likes to describe herself as a wandering cloud that romances with the sky, lost yet free.

9. Believe

If I were to listen to people, "Trust the universe", they'd say
Wordly things don't happen by chance
It's like an act on stage at play
On ornate floors where people dance.

....

A stardust collection of people
Riding high on life
Like some dilapidated prequel
To an un-ending soul strife.

....

But no matter what, don't lose faith
When the world clammers you down
Waiting in the infinite abyss, your future wraith
Don't get scared or frown.

....

But laugh a hearty laughter
And flash your sparkly smile
Confidence is what you should chase after
The chase would be worthwhile.

- Gauri Shukla

10. I'd Follow You Into The Dark

If I were to die someday
I'd follow you into the dark
The scent of your memories lighting the way
Throughout the journey upon which I'd embark.

....

I'd swim through endless chasms
And bear any kind of body wretching spasms
I'd strip the whole of purgatory naked stark
To follow you into the dark.

....

I have missed you too much for too long
Now death seems to be the only escape
The dream of having you in my arms again, I cannot prolong
No matter what the case.

....

Dreaming or awake,
Alive or dead,
I've looked for you without a break
In the ghostly kingdoms that I daily tread.

....

If Heaven and Hell decide
That they both are satisfied
No blinding lights
Or gates of white
No scorching damnation
Or constant suffocation
I'd follow you into the dark.

- Gauri Shukla

11. Time-Travel

If I were to ever time travel in this life,
I know exactly the memories I'd bring back.
I'd love to end my twenty-year-old inner strife
And heap all those long-lost memories in a solid stack.

....

Firstly, I'd go to my childhood home
And hug the mango tree that I used to climb.
I'd take a picture and kiss its brome
And lay under its cool shade until it's go-time.

....

Then I'd go back to the time when Jenny was still alive
Oh! How I'd love to see her wagging away her tail happily
Forgetting all those haunting shadows of trying to get her to
revive
I'd hug her and kiss her and hold her to my chest tightly.

....

If I were to go back in time
I'd tell papa to spend more time with me.
I'd ask him to read me books and tales of fairies and monsters
grime
I'd hug him tighter just to let him know that he's my eternal tree.

....

I'd try not to get angry with ma a lot
Even after she gives me a lashing or two
I'd try to understand her feelings before I began to plot
A devious plan to make her feel blue.

....

I'd go back to the childhood that was pure
Sans thoughts of dwelling in the past or staggering into the
future
It was the present moment that was the lure
Untainted with the ugly lines of a bodily suture.

....

Most of all, I'd tell myself that the road ahead is not easy
It's full of rocks and ridges and turns of uncertainty
But hold your head high
Because that's the only thing that, to happiness, will take you
nigh.

- Gauri Shukla

12. Un-ending Chasms

If I were to do something for myself,
I'd make myself more digestible,
Try to make myself easy to love
And easy to heal.

....

With every passing minute, I feel my heartbeat spike
A familiar rush of blood to the irreparable cold veins
A constriction in the throat like a boulder that wouldn't roll off.
A silent sob that is stifling the airway, gurgling deep at the base
of my throat.
I push it down. Swallow it.

....

A dilation of the pupils as the irises take on a dull dead hostility
that I'm way too familiar with.
I can hear the blood pumping its way to my brain.
Each crevice, every ridge, silently filled with the sticky warm red
liquid.
The sound is deafening.

....

Where are the tears though?
I feel them forming but I don't feel them falling.

Mountain after a mountain of stifled, choked, unwanted
emotions,
Ready to burst through the seam of my body.
....
I have an urge - a disgusting, horrid, all-powerful urge to create
an opening on the patches of my tainted skin.
Tainted with sin.
Tainted with the touch of razor-sharp metal.
A skin that goes numb to the touch of anything human.
A panorama of dark shadows on the almond hue of the skin.
....
I can feel my heart getting ripped open.
Each vessel holding it together, torn apart like soot from burnt
paper.
Each bone protecting it, broken and strewn like miserable twigs
after a deadly tempest.
I can feel the pain singeing my body like a white-hot iron
brandishing.
But only for a moment.
....
It comes and goes like waves on a barren seashore.
It retreats, slowly fading into the dark taverns of my body it
coiled from
Only to strike again after a second of momentary relief.
Wave after wave of un-ending, eternal gloom, eternal doom.
....
Galloping through my veins

The chasm soundlessly expands everytime you touch me
There, in the center of that silence is loneliness so profound,
The word itself has no meaning.

....

It feels like standing on a ledge, which has only enough space for
a pair of feet.
Endless chasms all around, infinite solitude, and infinite
tempest.
A little shuffle of feet and I'd fall into the blackhole of doom.
There's not enough air. Why isn't there any air?

....

Breathe. Breathe. Breathe.
Wait for the numbness to take over.
Smile.
Carry on.
Live.
Survive.

– Gauri Shukla

Raman Singh

Raman Singh was born in the year 2001 in Haryana, India. He never did things to pass time, when he held on to a thing he gave himself completely to it. May it be playing basketball for nine years, may it be doing theatre, which also induced interest for literature. He is currently pursuing BA English Hons, from Delhi University, and is an important part of the theatre society. He has also acted in six theatrical productions and has himself written several short plays and stories. Not to forget his love for Hindi Literature, which has added new dimensions to his imaginations and in which he finds those values and thoughts which otherwise would've been too late to discover. If there is anything else which he loves, that is a cup of coffee. His notion of feeling content and happy is to have A cup of coffee with brownie while reading a book.

13. Starcity

If I were to
Build a city of mine
That would be amidst
Stars of the night.
Boundaries marked by them
Narrow streets lightened by them
Sparkling atmosphere spread by them
And
With the Moon guarding the city
It would be the safest city
For the lovers of the night.

– Raman Singh

14. A Life Without Desires

If I were to
throw away my desires
I would have had sleep during nights
and
Guilt free days
In my Life.

....

But desires don't leave you
Until you leave them
They stay with you
Until you stay with them
So
You keep on feeding them
Time and Energy
And they become the Voldemort
Of your life story
And effortlessly
You would be fooled into serving the powerful man
But all you would be
One step away from turning into sand

– *Raman Singh*

15. To Be With You

If I were to
Escape my room
I would choose
To be with you.
To be with you,
Closed eyes
Arms tight
Hearing your heart beat
With my ear above it
Listening to what
My heart starts to live
Who was until dead
With anxieties all over his head
And at the joy of living again
Those tears start to cry
Which were hopeless during the days
And tired at nights
Of not seeing you
When I opened my eyes

- Raman Singh

16. Changing The World Dream

If I were to become an

Inventor

It would be of the morals, not the materials.

We need inventors like these

'Cause materials are present in abundance

By the people working in poor conditions

Going home late-night drinking a beer

Their wife shouts (out of care), "Oh my dear, why so late?"

In return, they slap their wives and break their child's changing-

the-world dream

'Cause we live with the immoral moral

How could a Man bear a Woman

Whose love is so sheer.

....

So we don't need repairments

We need inventions

To create the materials with truthful morals.

- Raman Singh

Khushi Kaushik

Khushi Kaushik, the author of 'Secret of room 333' is known for her flash fiction. She started writing her first book when she was 13, which is a very young age. She is 19 at present and is pursuing English literature from University of Delhi. Apart from being an author she is a poetess as well. Her compilation of romantic poems 'Shades of love' had a great readership. She is an eager learner who loves to take up new challenges and broaden her horizons.

17. Star-Crossed Lover

If I were to be anything
I'd be yours forever

....

I'd tell you what love is
From day to night
I'd hold you so close
Won't let you out of my sight

....

I'll show you what love is
Through body and soul
And not just by words
'Cause words can be foul

....

I'll make you feel what love is
By pouring all the emotions
Will talk my heart out to you
Won't leave you in confusions

....

If i really were to be yours, love
I'd give you the whole galaxy
But alas it's not real
You're mine only in my fantasy.

– Khushi Kaushik

18. His Last Pretence

If i were to be dead tomorrow
I'd come to again
I'd leave all our sorrow
And let you break my heart again

....

But oh i forgot about she
She who is yours now
With whom you cheated on me
And i couldn't know how

....

I know it's been decades
But my love still lives on
I can bear more heartaches
But can't let you forgone

....

I want to see your pretence
As i am to face my last breath
Take your fake love in abundance
And lie and wait for death

....

Asleep in your lap in a blink
Lying there i suddenly think

GRAIL

....

Paradise i foreseen
But in life i got none
Hell is where i have till now been
So i won't fear to go to one

– Khushi Kaushik

19. Free

If I were to be free
And owned by none
I could have owned the sun

....

I would have feared none
And do whatever pleases me
I would have always been on a run
To be who I want to be

....

I'd see the streets at night
And wander till the dawn
I might even take a flight
To discover why i am born

....

I would have fought battles
Without fearing what they say
I'd be unchained to rattles
And allowance of me what I may

....

But they cut off my wings
Fearing I would flee
And finally, be free...

– Khushi Kaushik

Jeevasha Batra

Jeevasha, a student of English literature, was born in the food capital of India, New Delhi. She is a keen learner and observer. She is enthusiastic about exploring different facets of life." Expectations: A Tragical Road to Misery" is her first work wherein she has shared relevant incidents of her life that explain why having expectations is nasty and how it is like gambling your emotions for a person's future actions. Her work is a reflection of the lessons learned through her experiences which has enabled her to be free of expectations and strive for a life free of any biases and suppositions.

20. Why be afraid of Death?

If I were to die,
I wouldn't sigh,
Because it's a reality you can't escape, even if you try.
You see, I won't lie
Cause it's the destiny you can't deny.

....

Do you know how people die?
Some through vehicles that pass by,
Well, others for passion that make them cry;
Sometimes it is by choice but sometimes it is pure fate.

....

Fear not my friend,
Cause you are not the only one in this cage;
Be it a common man or a celeb,
Your day will come whether it is in March or in Feb.

- Jeevasha Batra

21. If I Were A Boy

If I were to be a boy,
I would roam around fearlessly at night,
Without my Mom daunting at me in spite.
I wouldn't beat my sister at times
As if it was alright.
She is a human who has rights
And if you hurt her, then you're gonna pay the price.

....

I would not wear makeup
Cause it's the beauty of mind that makes up;
I would not do household chores as if I was doing a favour,
Because it's time you need to wake up.

....

If I were a boy,
I would not pretend to be strong
Cause it's the society that's got it all wrong
Everyone's got a heart That aches
Because we are all capable of making mistakes.

- *Jeevasha Batra*

Rahul Jha

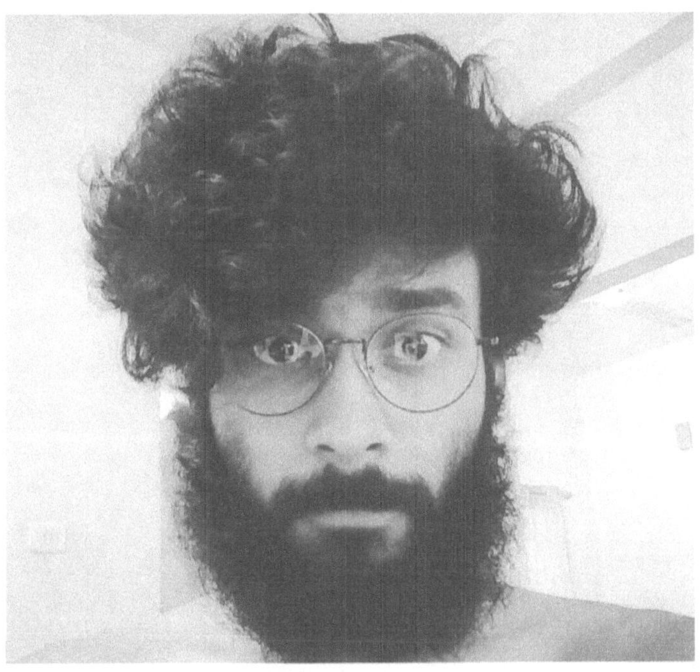

Standing still in the conundrum of inebriation; I write. To learn certain things and to unlearn the rest. Paraplegic. Confused. Curious. In this particular order. On a regular afternoon, I look at my life in the third person and get increasingly agitated at how

things continue to reveal themselves.

22. Aléf

If I were to die
Which must be soon
Let me be the first letter
of the modest Persian alphabet

....

Start covering me up
From the top right corner
And timidly move leftward
Like blots of ink on a Venetian palm

....

And if I wake up
(which must be scandalous)
Unstring our olden vocabulary -
borrowed, moldy, and putrescent
Like splinters of old frankincense
In a stained knapsack

....

Gently, gently, ever so gently
Count me the days of the moon

....

And with that very subliminal simplicity
On the ill-fashioned tombstone

write: aléf

– Rahul Jha

• 64 •

23. Vermilion

If I were to recall it,
I'd say, like everything else
This happened a long time back
And since it has been so so long
I don't remember if I remember it happening

....

It had to be you
Or someone who now I think was you,
Your inquisitive fingers coming to rest
On the bridge of my nose as I lay there

....

There's a possibility
That it never happened
But only if I could remember it happening
It'll take away half of the miseries of my life

....

The greys in your hair
The freckles on your arm
The vermilion in the parting of your hair;
Mother- I no longer want to remember any of it
But I never could forget any of it in the first place

....

And all of what happens to me
And all that brings me back your memories,
Is because I'm looking at my reflection in the mirror;
Which, like your memories, is hazy, botched up, and bludgeoned

– Rahul Jha

Shruti Upadhyay

An undergrad student of literature from DU who loves to read and has a strong passion for writing. I have a blog on which I post my writings. On normal days you would find me scrolling endlessly, reading, playing with dogs, and talking to plants. I am a professional over-thinker and procrastinator. I believe writing makes me strong and helps me to fight the injustice that prevailed. The poems submitted are an experiment of jotting down my thoughts swirling by.

You can contact me at -shrutiupadhyay1504@gmail.com

24. Witch of Macbeth

If I were to be of the witches of Macbeth,
I would seek a therapist for me
Learn the art of self-love and optimism.
Would haul the world and tell them I am not crazy
Or a witch but an independent woman which you are scared of.
Would choose a vocation and break this male-centric world.
Would soar high in the sky, not with the devil wings
But through the success achieved.

- Shruti Upadhyay

25. Intruder

- Shruti Upadhyay

26. Would I?

If I were to be this, I always thought.
Would it change how am I?
Would the sounds of my parent coming to my room
Would not scare me?
Would I be ever able to talk with him without
Shuttering and shaking?
Would I get rid of my anxiety and stop the art of people-pleasing?
Would I be able to say 'no'?
I closed my eyes with these thoughts.

- Shruti Upadhyay

27. Eyes of Earth

If I were to be the eyes of Earth,
What would I see?
Will it evoke catharsis
Or would I shriek?
My eyes flew open with sudden chaos,
I saw them in front of me,
Pinning him to my flat stomach,
Struck a hard blow across his face.
I was bathed in the gush of blood,
Reminding me of old times
When streams used to flow over me
Leaving me with offsprings of flowers.
The world has changed,
Closed my eyes
And never opened again.

- Shruti Upadhyay

28. Interjection with Furies

If I were to I would summon the furies
Are you just confined to those enchanting-looking books which
hold the bitter truth?
Did you just want the glorification and turned back to the
injustice that prevailed?
Where were you when he killed her own mother, in front of my
very own eyes?
Have you sold your serpent's to the charmer,
And constricted yourself as a mythological figure and hid into the
arms of the myths?

- Shruti Upadhyay

Ananya Dutta

Ananya Dutta is an amateur who is currently trying to strive in the field of creative writing. She is a student studying English at Bharati College, University of Delhi, and grooves at every beat of music of the pop genre. Ananya Dutta hails from a small town called Sivasagar in Assam and is fond of lexical diction and a book that underscores anything real never fails to delight her.

You can reach out to her on -

YourQuote –Alpha Matthews (Anyston Sighs)

Writco - Ananya Dutta

STORYSTAR – Alpha

StoryMirror – Ananya Dutta

Goodreads – Ananya Dutta

Miraquill – alpha3

Email ID – ananyastrong@gmail.com

29. A Fatal Folly

If I were to let myself voice what has been so palpable right inside my chest, would these hands I hath seize the chance; Carved would be a portrait in words of true wisdom for hath my mind been too ordinary and too laudable art thou.

Do my eyes now behold this spell, ah! such a heavenly diatribe art thou capable of - was I torn with every syllable that did thine tongue form.

'Tis a shame. Thou find me here still.

"Have I no shame?" enquire I myself - must I answer thee as thou ask me the same.

Drowsy art my eyes now, yet chagrin mauls more significantly.

May I divulge it once more - the labyrinth has that been so intact all this while?

Alas! fears my heart. Demands it that ascertain I foremost if any design of a chisel thy mind bears; I will ask for ask I must. Lackaday! such terror surrounds now! yet, aloof it lies inside this body of mine. Has thy presence been so sweet for it to be detest all bitterness at the utmost.

Strange how it envisages the state of thy heart. Ah! foul foolishness! Stench is it that pollutes my breath. Wonder I if thou smell it too. Can you tell?

*Did an hour elapse and soon were days passing me by. Swiftly
did they come and leave in just a blink - intensified is my
remorse for this time that I still waste;
Will I ever learn to be in a shape of thy fancy - with locks tied in
single a chignon of my hair, my chemise taken into fugitive by
the apparel thou wove for must I keep my own skin, and wrap
my waist because oh! how gross is that curvature have I also
come to behold? Can thou tell?
If I were to tell thou the truth, would I do it with pleasure of
every kind.
If I were to show my edge of the spectacle, would I render my
sight blinded. Might thou then infer the red on the surface. Has
it been right on the surface since so long my dear. Why can't thou
see?
Unregenerate as is thine perception, unruffled art thou to me -
would a man not let his sister perish in ashes black otherwise!
How rash, how perfidious, how untouched hath thee been whilst
all my daylight seeped that from betwixt nimbuses grey!
What a folly! what a folly! Ah! what a folly for heaven's sake!
hath I been all on a parallel time. 'Tis a shame, is it not dear?
Art the heavens making silver lines in the sky, Followed by
roaring sounds,
So loud, could be heard and seen wondrously high, With bits of
colossal shaking pounds.*

- Ananya Dutta

30. There's My Brother Away

If I were to gaze at the pit of soil - brown underneath the auburn hue, would I do it outright for an hour until were thee out of sight. This scenery was beautiful all around the more you see.

The zephyr a gale, the sun my moon, the clouds my stars - ah! What a spectacle for some eyes to see as long as they could see! Yet alas! was my notice so captivated, or confiscated as brother art thou of mine (If I say, will thee mind?)

Did I behold the water in the pit run grubby.

'Twas a sight I disliked. I will tell thou - I will hurl this fear in mine elsewhere and stride to say that I will tell thou my heart.

But if I say something, will thee listen?

"Two indeed, me and my sister.", harked I quite right. A pain of its own kind.

Has it not been thirty suns and thirty moons dear? Tell me, am I wrong?

Has it been hot summer days with rain sporadic in the past and hours on end like we must pass them as consciously as would we breathe in each second of the lapse? Must I know before I tell, am I wrong dear?

Ah! what a penance for me to pay!
Dare as I also may, I will probe anyway for hath I probed so
long. Oh my heart of blessing, my mother's peace on Earth, was
a soupcon of anything there that thou paid?
Alas! Stand thee so quiet, but this assent from thy edge is so loud
that deafened will my ears be.
Deafened should they hath been, could I keep thee still.
Thus here I say, if I were to ponder over a sight, or yonder the
sky, would I stare straight into the black of the universe for a
lifetime.
"Why?" thee ask! Ah! Is it extraordinary for my mind to have
someone behold everything, yet nothing at all. Is the latter for me
I suppose. I must not blame you.
Lackaday! Ah! am I so doomed my brethren! Art thou leaving
now.
'Tis thy departure that is ripping apart my blessing so naked!
What a sacrilege! how blasphemous!
God, will I ever be pardoned for alas yet again, can I not say "
'tis not mine in any way" for do these vicissitudes stick to my
skin as black a shade does with the night sky when all is asleep
and sweetly in dream? Holy Lord, will I ever be pardoned?
My brother parts too soon now, and still I gaze at the pit both
black and brown.
Is it not an admiration, but a preference to beholding thou leave
my side.
My brother is away and away further with time.

Hath I sought a place for thee - Will thou rest in the blind spot of my eye - tiny and insignificant, sensitive and thus, cosseted - whilst I float away in the flotsam of a sea.

• 81 •

- *Ananya Dutta*

Tushita Aster Paul

Tushita is a meritorious student who was also the President of the
Debate Society of her college. An ambitious and determined yogi,

she absolutely loves to read, especially if the genre is psychological thriller. From drawing mandalas to relax her mind to going on cycling trails, she loves to experiment and doesn't want to miss out on any opportunity that life throws at her. Learning new languages is another one of her hobbies. You might find her randomly clicking pictures of the sunset and the sky at any given time. Collecting fancy stationery is yet another of her guilty pleasures. An explorer who lives for anything and everything sweet, loves to bake, and listen to 90s Bollywood music.

31. You

If I were to know I would encounter you that night.
If only I foresaw it somehow.
But you happened.
As unannounced as a splash of rain on a bright sunny day.
You always had that gorgeous smile spread across your face.
Do you know how it made me do horrible things?
Things I wouldn't have even dreamt of committing.
You made me vulnerable and I did not like it.
Those eyes of yours saw right through me,
Accusing and disrespecting me more often than not.
I tried my best to please you.
But you? You were so difficult.
You compelled me to do this.
Oh man! You still look ravishing lying like that.
The red pool around you compliments your beautiful milky skin.
I wonder if I ever deserved you.
Maybe I didn't, that's why I sent you away.
But why aren't you smiling?
You're free now.
I'm sorry I couldn't inform you.
Just thought your end needed to be unannounced as well.

– Tushita Aster Paul

• 86 •

32. Belong

If I were to tell you, I don't know where I belong?
Leaving behind cities, states,
Moving place to place.
Trying to fit in,
To get accepted.
But wait, I need to shift again.
Pack up my bags,
To catch that plane.
A new day, an alien town.
I need to settle again,
Find a new set of faces.
Maybe it's the last time,
Guess these comrades will stay.
But wait.
Do I really belong here?
Cause these people sharing laughter,
Making memories,
They seem so far away.
Unreal like a mirage.
I guess,
I don't belong here either.
For I'll need to move,

GRAIL

To a new horizon.
Make a new home,
In a new world yet again.

– Tushita Aster Paul

Akrita

I am Akrita Sharma. I am pursuing a Master's course in Literature from Guru Nanak Dev University, Amritsar. A Thousand Splendid Suns by Khaled Hosseini caught my heart and paved my way into the world of books and from there on began my love for reading. I do not write to publish, so this is a first, and it needed a push, and that came from my sister Apra. Writing began as a way for me to express things that I could never say and that's how it always has been. My words are a part of me, I spill what I feel. I love through words, I live through words and I hope through words. And not that this is relevant to anything, or maybe it is and it came from a loved one so here goes nothing, ice-creams are my favorite things in the world and I secretly wish to be a penguin and search rocks with my forever soulmate.

33. If I Were To

If I were to have wings,
I would fly away across the continent all the way to you,
Only to catch a glimpse of you once more,
I would see you tuck yourself under the sheets a little
Tighter and play peek-a-boo with the sun as it rises through the
window,
Only to freeze the moment in time like polaroids do,
I would nudge the edges of your head ever so gently
And see you wake up and smile at me,
Only to re-live how autumn feels when it turns to spring,
I would wrap you in my arms and listen to your heart beating,
Only to crumble down and leave behind tears
Because I may never cross your paths again, only to lose sleep
Because I have so much of you in my heart,
Only to engrave it in me as a token of missing from you,
Only to carry it as a souvenir of depriving myself of the presence
of you,
Only to miss you more,
If I were to have wings,
I would always choose you.

- Akrita

34. I am you!

If I were to reverse the clocks again,
I would visit the twelve-year-old me,
I'd hug her tight and tell her we are going to make it through the
world just fine,
She'd look at me a bit dazed but then she would smile her
chipped tooth smile,
I would sing her songs for years to come,
A little bit of Scars to Your Beautiful,
A little bit of Who Says,
A little bit of Alag Aasmaan,
A little bit of Stay,
I'd hold her hand and sit with her,
I'd run through the fields with her and we'd climb the guava tree
in our maternal grandmother's home,
We'd dance and
She would tell me about all the things she did and how she will
forever be this way,
I'd smile, pat her head,
I'd listen, take it all in, the memories of the girl I used to be,
I wouldn't disclose anything because she deserves to be her own
woman,

But, I'd tell her to fall in love with herself before she gives her
heart away to the world,
Then, we would move on, look at the sky, watch it shift from
orange to blue only to end up in pitch black with a golden moon,
And I would point at the moon and tell her, even if everything
changes, you and him will always be the same,
People will come and go, and maybe hearts would break too,
some days would be hard, and maybe you'll lose your way too,
But whatever you share with the moon, will always stay with
you!
Her eyes would go wide and she'd ask how do you know?
I'd say that is because I am you.
She'd stop in her tracks,
I'd prepare to leave,
She'd choke in shock,
And I'd take the leap.

- Akrita

Nishita Sharma

I am Nishita Sharma a law student who constantly finds solace in poetry and rain. I always find myself rummaging through various sources to find words that make my interiors melt.

35. Poetic Embodiments

If I were to run around in circles
I'd weave poems about how
The cassette plays Teri Fariyad in a circle
Winter morning and dewy leaves
I received your message
And I am shivering "I'm coming back to take away my
belongings"
I hold your flannel shirt in my lap
My tears mixing up with its pale green color
Your eyes are also green na?
Your message is melting on my finger tips like a cold ice
surrendering to the warm tears
You are coming back
Yes
How would you like me?
Would you hug me?
Or you'd just pretend not to look in my eyes
Should I make your special chai
Or you've stopped drinking chai also?
Like you stopped listening to The 1975 after you left me

....

Do you remember my Playlist?

Do you still have it?
Do you shuffle it?
Or You have just deleted
Maybe?
You are coming back
I should wear that dress you gifted on our first anniversary
Or I should act like a stranger " mujhse kuchh teri nazar puchh
rahi ho jaise"
The question inside my heart are bewitched
But I must hold them back
They'd just escape my tongue and
You'd leave
But
You are coming back
So maybe stay a night
We'd play Apocalypse whole night
And I'd serve you your favorite wine
Do you know I started smoking?
I'm belittled, with every second going by I'm teaching myself to
walk past those familiar smiles that familiar voice and those
familiar eyes
For they are closed for me " meri har saans tere naam likhi ho
jaise" "waqt ke pass lateefein bhi hain marham bhi hain"
I learnt to weave poems at an age of 9
Because I was scared to let the world hear my voice
So I'd create yarns and trap words in them and with my fingers
sew them together

SWARNIKA

And I called it beautiful
My first poem about you embodied love
And my last embodied pain
So tonight if you'd say have I moved on
I'll write you another poem embodying both

- Nishita Sharma

36. For The Moments You Can't Remember

If I were to travel back to the memories
I'd remember the one time you asked me
A truth and a lie
I love you
I miss you
Silence and tears intermingling
Longing like a landscape of hands too afraid to make fists
Too scared to utter words of affirmations, so you whisper in
between sighs
Hoping the goddess beyond the clouds hears you
Cementing all the violent memories to prevent them from
hurting you
Death clinging to my lips like the lingering after-effect of kisses
planted after months of desertion
The silence and the farcical loneliness in your eyes holding back
the longing at the corners of your mouth
When they ask us to stop loving each other
Should we ask why?
Or is it the smell of the sea in your shirt's pocket
That's keeping me unhinged

A dim light at a distance
Is it enough?
Do we like enough?
You let the sunlight fall through the blinds
And you break down on your kitchen cabinet
Holding my hands close to your lips
And you mutter prayers hoping to fall or rise again
In the slivers of the moon
A truth and a lie
I love you
I miss you.

– Nishita Sharma

37. For Hunger And Nothing Less

If I were to tell you how things ended
I'd tell you that
The end of things wasn't an apocalyptic ordeal
It was the silence that stayed intact between us
12 heartbreaks and 7 syllables
A mouth full of blood
The city skies engulfing the rooftops
While we sat there dangling our legs
Unaware and naive
We opened our windows in the face of untoward storms
We lighted candles at dawns
Waited in longing, our voices taken away
Holy things are better left untouched
I swear my lips have quivered, mere inches away from yours
The luminescence echoes and moonlight
Reverberates in our room
Periwinkle blankets,
My fingers around your wrist.
It hurts you say, to come home
And yet I see you tracing the outlines of my face

Carefully, as if abstaining from unleashing something untamable
Remnants of memories heavy on your eyelids
You named your hometown after a dead language,
Now no one else has the words
You are love, with its knees bruised and its sleeves rolled up
You are forgiveness with a knife in your hands
You are terribly melancholic and lonely
You have graveyards inside of you, and you are haunted by my
familiar touch
You look up and the sky is silver
[your first experience of abandonment like first rain in droughts]
like an ache, like a wound afresh
You've wanted to cut yourself open, and let it all out
But somewhere in that, I know you're warm
I know you're safe

....

You swallow yourself whole and leave me with chapped lips and
a half-torn heart
And my home has been silent since
Somewhere, along the edges
I let you go
And somewhere else
I am learning how to come home
I am relearning how to come home

- Nishita Sharma

38. Beyond The Milky Way - A Tale Of Being Peripheral

If I were to tell you a beautiful yet tragic story. I'd tell you about how

My mother met her first love in the canteen

(he looked at her like she was the sun soothing his cold skin)

Says it ended abruptly

Like a sudden abrupt appearance of a yellow flower on your way back home

You can't keep it because it looks better away from you in its original habitat

Is that why the idea of falling in love with my own self seems so distant

On dealing with dearth of self-love the reconciliation of being visited by my own absence

Love is resting somewhere in the middle of a lavender field

resting its feet on the violet trails of undisturbed serenity

Saving itself from falling deep into not - echoing tranches

Somber walls made of fragile veins

It's not time

Not yet not yet

You can be everything you want
Do any of those dreams include me?
Or am I just a fading memory
It wasn't a dream that we met
Was it?
I have loved you so much that I forgot what you look like
I only remember the weightlessness of my bones from when you
first saw me
Taste of bittersweet memories still fresh on my sugar burnt
tongue
My eyes still finding a way to carve you in the back of my head
Nothing
Not yet not yet
On these days it's hard to love the sunset or the wind making me
feel alive
It's hard to let go
I can't remember you
You seem like a patchwork of contradictions
I believe you could find a thousand naked metaphors about my
sorrow in the way I do my hair
Or the way I make my tea
Or the way I sit at my desk and sleep till 3 AM
Or the way I place flowers in the middle of the books and on the
mirrors I remove my make up in
Or the way I sigh after breathing too long
But I could give you a list
A list of all the times you hurt me

GRAIL

I could itemize you a letter of tragedies you unleashed on me
with every wrecking word
I am still terrified of dark
But more terrified of the light where I would find a face just like
yours
A face that screams familiarity
And I would fall in love again
And I am afraid I'll fall
I'm afraid I'll run towards love and it would be just a step back
from catching me
So I don't
Not yet not yet
And yet this is again stitched with the threads hanging out of my
heart broken apart from yours
I will stop running and will let people in but
For hunger and nothing else
At dawn, in silence I rose again
Pressing against the silence,
My Ghost - thin shadow coursing through the walls
Teach me to breathe again

- Nishita Sharma

Ritika Tyagi

Ritika Tyagi is currently a student majoring in Mathematics from the University of Delhi. She has always been a huge fan of rhymes but was never much interested in literature. Instead, she was always into music. She was deeply influenced by how some songs managed to move a soul by using the simplest of words, and that inspired her to write. In the November of 2020, she wrote her first poem, and since then she has been writing poems inspired by people, and situations around her. She mostly tries to tell a story through her poems using rhymes. She believes that the reader should have fun while reading her poems, that her poems should sound like a song in readers' minds.

39. My Story

If I were to tell my story,
I'd attract the audiences of others.
Not because I'm a good seller,
But because I've known nothing better, nothing worse.

....

It's the kind of story that will make you cry.
Where the hero dies, and the villain survives,
Where people fake to become your allies,
Where some lies become truths, and some truths become lies.

....

It's a story too long.
Too long for me to fit in a song.
It could've been nice to see people sing along
To something that highlights the wrong.

....

Because when will we stop this culture of 'a happy ending'?
Till when will we keep turning a blind eye to the sorrow?
Why do we make our children believe that bad things only
happen to bad people,
When we ourselves don't know what will happen tomorrow?

....

This story is mine,

But a thousand others have experienced something of a similar
kind.
Some don't care and want to leave it all behind.
And some who cannot but want to tell, are always trying.

....

Those few people want the world to know
Some things that have always been ignored.
But it's hard for them to show-
Their scars to this world,
So they just don't.

....

And stories like these end in vagueness,
Just like they started.
People are always looking for happiness,
So stories like mine are often disregarded.

- Ritika Tyagi

40. The Ruined Love

If I were to yell back at you that day,
I wouldn't have to face any of this.
The betrayal, the insult, the forced kiss.
The hurt, the pain, the silent cries,
I wouldn't have to live with any of your lies.

....

If I never forced myself to stay,
I would have been alive.
Ever since I met you,
I only lived, never had a life.
My soul died the day you touched it,
And ever since then, I've only felt disgusted.

....

If only I had walked away,
My body wouldn't have suffered this much.
This much, and all in the name of love.
My mind didn't have to bear all that,
If only I had left and never came back.

....

If I were to yell back at you that day,
Life would not have been the same.
But I didn't, hoping you'd change.

Because once upon a time, we adored each other,
Because once upon a time, you said I was your lover.

– Ritika Tyagi

Thank You!

Dear Reader,

We'd like to thank you for reading this poetical anthology. We hope you appreciated the work presented here. In case you have any feedback or would like to reach us regarding the book, kindly reach us at swara@nrityanganakalakendra.com. Your input is valued and we'll love to hear from you.